GW00601274

One-Sided Triangle

A play

Stephen Smith

Samuel French—London
New York-Toronto-Hollywood

ONE-SIDED TRIANGLE

First performed by Waterbeach Community Players at Waterbeach School, on Friday, 13th March 1992, with the following cast:

Mike	Alex McLauchlin
Brian	Martin George
Sarah	Caroline Harris

Directed by Stephen Smith
Designed by Mark Easterfield and Janet Crack
With the assistance of Julie Petrucci, Eddie Curtis, Jane Butcher, Martin Andrus, Alan Dean, Chris Shinn and Kalaya Wilderspin

ONE-SIDED TRIANGLE

The garden of a small hotel bar in the northern Thai city of Chiang Rai

Along the back are various plants, with a spirit house, adorned with Buddha statues, positioned C. R *is a white table with beer bottles on it. Two chairs are by the table and a hold-all under the chair* L. *Inside the hold-all is an English language newspaper, e.g.* Bangkok Post *or* The Nation. L *is another set of table and chairs. The bar entrance is* L, *the garden entrance is* R

As the CURTAIN *rises, Mike, a lean unshaven man wearing a short sleeved shirt and trousers, is pacing up and down smoking nervously*

Brian enters. He is older, smaller, and fatter. He is wearing a cap, a T-shirt and shorts

Mike So?
Brian Flight landed thirty minutes late. (*He sits down and takes the newspaper from the hold-all to read*)

Mike looks anxiously at his watch

Don't worry, she'll be here soon. Most likely hanging on for dear life as a kamikaze tuk tuk hurtles towards us at this very moment. Poor sod, they must be the most uncomfortable form of travel designed by man. (*He pauses*) Been on a camel?

Mike (*still pacing*) No.

Brian That must be the most uncomfortable form of travel designed by nature. Getting off is the worst, drop like a stone. (*He pauses*) Mind you, elephants aren't a lot better. Do you know the best way to get off an elephant?

Mike What I want to know is why she had to come here in the first place.

Brian I told you they got stroppy about the visa. She couldn't get it sorted until after I had left last night. So she has had to fly up this morning.

Mike Why?

Brian Well we couldn't have you traipsing around northern Thailand any longer without a passport, could we?

Mike No, why did they get stroppy?

Brian I don't know. I suppose they smelt a rat and you know what happens once they smell a rat: the price rockets. Luckily, you're dealing with pros. We know how to play it cute. Sarah's an expert. She knows how to walk away, tell them you'll think about it, let them sweat a little.

Mike (*agitatedly*) I haven't got time to let some corrupt official sweat a little.

Brian Look, it worked all right. No worries. You want to take some money home with you, don't you?

Mike I'd also like to get home in one piece. All I've asked for is a clean passport to get out legit. Is that too much to ask? I thought you could get anything in this country if you had the money?

Brian You can, but it takes time. These officials know you can easily get a new passport complete with the works on the black market. So as soon as we start offering above the going rate, they get suspicious, and then the proverbial hits the fan. "Either this falang's a prat or he doesn't want the mob involved. Perhaps we'd better check." You want that?

Mike What do you think?

Brian Like them, I think it's a bit fishy why you wouldn't settle for a forged passport like all the rest. And why I have to come all this way to collect you and take you to Bangkok in a minibus. It's a bloody twelve hour drive. What have you been doing up here?

Mike Business.

Brian That's what they all say. (*He pauses*) I bet it's carvings.

Mike Carvings?

Brian The carved wood. The teak. Beautiful stuff, I've got to admit. Although what someone wants with a wooden elephant half the life-size is beyond me. They'd need a jumbo to take it back. (*He laughs*)

Mike Yes.

Brian Smuggling carved teak furniture, that's your game, isn't it? Worth thousands back home. Naughty to the environment and difficult to get out of the country. Probably already been caught, so that's why you need another passport. Thought I was stupid, didn't you?

Mike The thought crossed my mind.

Brian That's why you need a minibus.

Mike You did hire it in Pattaya?

Brian Of course I did. I've even got "Top Thailand Tours" plastered all over it, as requested. Very original, I must say.

Mike The idea is not to stand out, it's to blend in with the tourist trade.

Brian Most tourists don't travel to Bangkok in a minibus. They take the luxury coach service. Reclining seats, food, movie— they even have hostesses.

Mike I am paying enough, aren't I?

Brian I suppose so, but it will be extra if I'm driving any smuggled gear.

Mike (*angrily*) Save the comments and do as you're told, or you won't be getting anything. (*He stares at the entrance to the bar*)

Brian (*getting up annoyed and going over to Mike*) Look, I don't have to be here, you know. I don't have to take this from you. I've got a perfectly good thing going for me in Pattaya. This is only *petty cash*. I can walk away, I can.

Mike If your bird doesn't turn up within the next five minutes, it'll be me that'll be doing the walking.

Brian (*retreating to his chair*) She'll be here. No worries. (*He pauses*) Look, how about a beer to calm your nerves?

Mike I want to keep a clear head.

Brian You have got it bad, haven't you? Don't worry, they can be bribed, you know.

Mike Who?

Brian The police. Leave all the talking to me. Not ivory, is it?

Mike No.

Brian Good. That would be costly, and I like elephants. Can't feel the same about trees as you do for animals, can you?

Mike (*joining Brian at the table*) It's not the police I'm worried about.

Brian Oh, that sounds more serious.

Mike You should try it some time.

Brian I've taken my share of risks here, you know.

Mike What? Running a bar on a tourist visa? Not exactly James Bond, is it?

Brian (*pausing, then taking a swig from a beer bottle*) They made one of those James Bond films here, you know. Down in Phuket. *Man With The Golden Gun*. You know the one with the funny shaped rocks coming out of the sea.

Mike Taxi driver, were you?

Brian What?

Mike Back in England?

Brian How did you know?

Mike Educated guess.

Brian (*getting up*) Just trying to make conversation. It would look bloody suspicious if we had sat here without saying anything.

Pause

Mike Sure this girl is kosher?

Brian Sarah? Oh, yes. She's up to her eyeballs in debt.

Mike I thought she was a pro.

Brian That's what makes her a pro in this game. She hasn't got any choice.

Mike But isn't in the embassy staff?

Brian No, freelance. (*Sarcastically*) Went to India to find herself. Got into Buddhism and ended up here. Married a Thai who traded her in for a new model a few years later, and now she makes her living as a translator.

Mike So how did she get me a new passport?

Brian Got a thing going with the Military Attaché, lucky lady. He can clear passport applications, no questions asked. Covert operations and all that.

Mike And what's her story?

Brian About why she needs a passport?

Mike Yes.

Brian You are someone she feels sorry for. Embassy wouldn't give your girlfriend a visa a couple of years ago, so you overstayed your welcome. Now you're worried the Old Bill are sniffing around, and without a new passport it's deportation, a huge fine, or imprisonment. Not necessarily in that order.

Mike And he fell for that?

Brian Happens all the time. Let's face it, the Thais have got to be the best lookers in the world. Not difficult to fall in love out here. That's why I stayed. Except I wasn't stupid enough to let my visa run out. Hop, skip, and a jump down to Malaysia every three months, and you are home and dry.

Mike And you are still with her?

Brian No, she was too good for me. I didn't deserve someone like her. She gave me this. (*He shows Mike a golden Buddha hanging on his necklace*) When she left. Supposed to bring me luck and protection. Not too good a track record so far. Worth a bit—solid gold. Really impressed Sarah.

Mike What's your hold over her?

Brian She's lived here too long not to get heavily into gambling. You name it, she's into it. So when she came to Pattaya, a few weeks ago, looking for some action, I got to her and decided to cultivate her.

Mike So you don't really know much about her?

Brian Enough. I have a bar. I can spot a loser. Couldn't survive without losers.

Mike And what makes you think you're not a loser?

Brian You came to me, remember. I'd say you should think yourself lucky that I fancied a trip up north. A bit of daytime for a change.

Mike Lucky, am I?

Sarah enters hurriedly. She is a plain looking woman in her thirties

Sarah Sorry I'm late.

Brian No worries, darling.

Sarah Everything is in the envelope: passport and life story. Who wants it?

Brian (*sitting down again to read his paper*) He does. I've already got my passport and life story.

Sarah (*handing the documents to Mike*) You are Paul Weaver, a workwear salesman from Croydon. First trip to Thailand.

Standard four days in Bangkok, eight in Phuket. Won it in a sales promotion.

Mike I am a lucky sod.

Sarah Not so lucky. On a day trip to Koh Samui your passport was stolen. British Embassy have supplied a new passport, and Thai Ministry of Foreign Affairs have issued a visa. By the way, you didn't really need a visa.

Mike I know.

Sarah Only stays over fifteen days require a visa.

Mike I know.

Sarah It's just that I was led to believe you were leaving as soon as possible.

Mike Then you were led to believe wrong.

Brian (*looking up from his paper*) You are staying longer now?

Mike Perhaps.

Sarah Whatever. You requested a visa and we obtained one. It's valid for two months. I hope that is long enough.

Mike Plenty.

Sarah Good. Then you should have no problem leaving the country.

Brian Unless he gets quizzed about the finer points of British workwear. (*He goes to her and slaps her on the backside*) Great job, sweetheart. Told you she was the best.

Mike (*studying the passport*) Yes.

Sarah (*annoyed at Brian*) Thank you. Now if I could have my fee, I have a return flight to catch.

Mike Already?

Sarah Yes.

Mike Only one flight to Bangkok today?

Sarah No. Why?

Mike As you've come all this way, I thought you might want to see the sights.

Sarah I'm not a tourist.

Mike (*prowling behind them menacingly*) No, of course not. Pity though: very interesting part of the country. The Golden Triangle of Thailand, Burma, and Laos—meeting on the Mekong river. The stuff of adventure stories. We could have all gone out on a boat in the middle of no-man's land. Or should I say no-person's water?

Brian (*peevishly*) What are you playing at, Mike? I thought you were in a hurry.

Mike I am, but why is Sarah?

Sarah It's not good for me to be seen in this part of the country.

Mike Why's that?

Sarah I think that is obvious.

Mike Better to be seen in a gambling den, I suppose.

Brian Stop mucking about, Mike. Pay the poor girl. She's done everything you asked.

Mike Why don't you? It was you I struck the deal with and the deal is to get me safely out of the country. From the South, not from the North. I don't want to go back to where I've already been, do I?

Sarah Been where?

Brian Does it really matter?

Sarah Of course it bloody matters. The border with both countries has a habit of being closed.

Brian It's too late to worry about that now.

Mike Rather naïve, your girl, Brian, and I thought she was a pro. I'd pay her off before she learns too much.

Brian I don't understand what's going on here. Are you trying to get out of paying? Because if you are, I've got to warn you I don't take too kindly to coming all this way without getting a result. If you are going to play silly buggers with me, I'll have the passport back and you can fend for yourself.

Brian goes for the passport, but Mike walks past him

Mike Don't get hot under the collar, Brian. I didn't realize that this little excursion was going to give you financial problems. I thought it was only petty cash. (*He casually sits down at table* L)

Brian I don't carry my petty cash around with me, do I? As Sarah has done you the courtesy of bringing up the passport personally, I would have thought you'd be grateful enough to pay her COD. I don't think that is too much to ask, do you?

Mike Sorry, but I do. I haven't done any deals with Sarah. I didn't want her here in the first place. It's your own incompetence to blame. Nothing to do with me. I'll pay COD when I get to Bangkok, and no sooner.

Brian This bloke obviously doesn't trust us, Sarah. I'm afraid I'll have to pay you when I get back to Pattaya.

Sarah I'm not that naïve. I've been to a lot of trouble to get that passport—I'm not getting stitched up.

Brian I won't stitch you up, you can trust me.

Mike Famous last words.

Brian What is the matter with you? Why are you doing this? A few minutes ago you couldn't wait to get out of here, now you seem to have all the time in the world.

Mike (*relaxedly*) A few minutes ago I didn't have my new passport.

Sarah Why didn't you tell me he hadn't paid you? I wouldn't have given him the passport if I'd known.

Brian I didn't think he'd behave like this. As far as I was concerned, all I was doing was trying to help a fellow Brit out. Now I find the bastard doesn't trust me an inch. I've never had any trouble with people like this in Pattaya.

Sarah We're not in bloody Pattaya now, are we? Real fish out of water you are. Typical man: all mouth in the bar, but no flaming use when it counts. What did you think you were doing, going on a Sunday School outing?

Mike Tell you what, I'm willing to do a deal.

Brian (*going up to him*) No we are not. Trying to get the price down, aren't you? I've sussed your little game. We've already done a deal.

Mike Right we have. Five thousand pounds on my safe departure from Don Muang Airport.

Sarah Five thousand pounds?

Brian I have my expenses.

Mike Don't squabble, children. I can make it considerably more, depending on which currency you want it in. The best currency around here is Super One Hundred Per Cent, Number One.

Long pause while the shock sinks in

Brian Drugs?

Mike Heroin. Most valuable in the business. Manufactured at Ta Kee Lek in Laos.

Sarah (*sitting at table* R*; gloomily*) I thought so, there is only one thing people come across the border with. You are a prat, Brian.

Brian I didn't know he'd come across the border. I thought he was smuggling carved furniture out of the country.

Sarah (*incredulously*) Carved furniture?

Brian (*embarrassed*) Well, they do make it here.

Sarah How did I ever get involved with you?

Mike It's the genuine stuff. Ask anyone which brand has all the lettering and artwork on the packaging in red. A circle with a deer's head in the top corners and tiger's head in the bottom corners. The word "Super" is written within the enlarged "One" and above the "One Hundred Per Cent".

Brian You've got it with you?

Mike I'm not as stupid as you.

Brian (*relieved*) Thank God for that.

Sarah (*getting up*) Brian, let's get out of here.

Brian How much have you got?

Mike Enough.

Sarah I said, Brian, let's go.

Brian Shut up. Where is it?

Mike Somewhere safe.

Brian So you've been into Laos and done a runner from this Ta Kee Lek place.

Mike In a manner of speaking.

Sarah (*pleading*) Please, Brian, let's go.

Brian What's the matter with you? He said he hasn't got it with him.

Sarah If you had seen what I have, you wouldn't be having this conversation.

Brian What?

Sarah Just trust me. Just leave before it's too late.

Brian What is it you've seen?

Sarah (*turning away from him*) Someone slowly die of heroin addiction. Such a horrible degrading death, you wouldn't wish it on your worst enemy.

Brian Where was this?

Sarah In Bangkok.

Brian In the slums?

Sarah No, at home.

Brian (*going up to her*) At home?

Sarah My husband.

Brian I thought you said he left you for another woman.

Sarah If people knew he was trying to go cold turkey they wouldn't have come anywhere near me. In the end I couldn't stand seeing him in such agony, so I gambled everything we had to satisfy his craving, until he died.

Brian (*putting his hand on her shoulders*) I'm sorry.

Sarah (*breaking away*) Just don't get involved. I learnt a lot about the whole sordid business while my husband was alive.

I know how these people's minds work. I know what he has in store for you.

Mike And what's that?

Sarah He's looking for mules.

Brian What?

Sarah Couriers, and you are an ideal candidate. You are certainly thick enough.

Brian Is all this true?

Mike I always find it fascinating. The year-long care and attention it takes to grow opium poppies; the skill involved in selecting the correct night on which to cut the pods. Cut too soon, and the sap will be runny and dribble to the ground; cut too late and the alkaloid in the sap will have become codeine, only one-sixth as potent as morphine.

Sarah Don't listen to him, Brian.

Mike When the harvest is complete, the opium is shaped into one-kilo bricks, wrapped in banana leaves, and tied with string. Later it will be taken to a crude jungle compound and reduced to morphine nuggets, and then to a laboratory to be processed into heroin.

Sarah And during the harvest, babies riding on their mothers' backs frequently die in their sleep from the opium fumes.

Mike Do you know how much the hill-tribes are paid for a kilo of raw opium? Two and a half thousand baht. But after it's refined into heroin, it's worth eighty thousand baht.

Brian What? About two grand!

Mike More or less, and I'm prepared to give you two and a half kilos instead of the five grand, if you want.

Brian No, I don't want. I'll just take the five grand, thank you.

Mike Unfortunately that is not an option. Not until I cash in the heroin.

Brian And when's that?

Mike When we get to Bangkok.

Brian I'm not going now and I want the passport back until you've got the cash.

Mike Do you think I'm not going to leave this place without a passport?

Brian Do you think I'm going to leave this place without being paid?

Mike You'd be far better off selling in Bangkok.

Brian If I have to sell, I sell it here.

Mike In Bangkok, it's worth five thousand pounds a kilo. Which would make your kilos worth twelve and a half thousand pounds. Not a bad profit for travelling with me. You can try and sell it here yourself, if you want, but without the contacts it's not advisable.

Brian But there are roadblocks everywhere.

Mike Why do you think I wanted an inconspicuous minibus? If we are stopped, it'll only get a cursory search. They only arrest foreigners on tip-offs.

Brian What if there's a tip-off on you?

Mike You don't have to come. We could part company here. Of course, if you don't fulfil your side of the bargain, you can hardly expect payment.

Brian Nowhere in the deal was a minibus stacked with heroin mentioned.

Mike (*smiling*) It's my luggage.

Brian This is ridiculous. I've been set up, haven't I?

Sarah If you had told me the truth, I could have saved you all this aggro. It's bloody obvious anyone coming over the border is into drugs.

Brian I suppose you do this every week: con some poor innocent sod like me.

Mike I wouldn't call you poor or innocent.

Brian Still a con though, isn't it?

Mike To set the record straight, this is a one-off, it's not a con.

A gamble, perhaps, but then life is a gamble. Either you leave empty handed, or you take risk coming to Bangkok. Entrepreneurs do it every day.

Brian But all they lose is money.

Mike Worst case scenario is a few years in prison. They don't execute foreigners here, and bargaining is possible if you have friends on the outside.

Brian Great, thanks a bunch. Got nothing to worry about at all then, have I?

Sarah It's Khun Sa's brand, isn't it?

Mike Well done.

Sarah That's why you couldn't risk a new passport from the black market.

Mike One phone call to the Thai Guild of Passport Makers.

Sarah But equally, you couldn't go around with the one he gave you, so it had to come from the British Embassy. And you need the visa as you intend to lie low in Bangkok for a while.

Mike While someone does a little errand.

Brian What are you on about?

Sarah Surely you know who Khun Sa is?

Brian Some sort of gangster.

Sarah The Opium Warlord of The Golden Triangle. Half Chinese, half Burmese, with a Thai wife thrown in to keep everyone happy. He has an army of fifteen thousand over the border and a network of informants here. Super One Hundred Per Cent is his brand. It was what my husband first took, while he could afford it.

Mike I take it all back, Brian. Your friend is not naïve at all.

Brian (*backing away*) No, no, this is way out of my league. I don't do drugs, I don't get involved with the mob. Perhaps you got the wrong impression. I'm not quite as big-time as I might have made out.

Sarah More like very small-time.

Brian More like.

Mike Don't panic, it's me he's after, not you. That's why I need you. I can't travel by public transport: he has all the stations and airports continually watched. I need you to drive me while I stay in the back. Until we get to Bangkok, where it's easy to hide.

Brian But what guarantee have I got that I'll get paid in Bangkok?

Mike None. Except I may need further help. Help that would be rewarded beyond your wildest dreams.

Sarah Brian, how can you seriously talk to a man like this after all that I've told you?

Brian Look, Sarah, I don't think you should wind him up. Perhaps it would be best if you caught that plane. I'll make sure you get your money, no worries.

Sarah You are going to help him?

Brian I don't know.

Sarah After all that I've said.

Brian Look, Sarah can go, can't she? She won't say anything. Will you, love?

Mike I'm not worried about her. She knows what will happen if I get caught. Don't you, darling? You are an accomplice, a member of the drugs gang that tried to help me get out of Thailand. "How was it again I got a new passport?" Try convincing them of any other story and they'd laugh in your face. Then again, the Thais like a good laugh, don't they, Brian?

Brian I'm sorry, Sarah, but it's too late.

Sarah (*grabbing him*) No, it isn't. Come with me now. Forget the money.

Brian I can't forget the money, Sarah. I've come all this way. Times aren't what they used to be. What with this AIDS business, Pattaya is going for a more family image. Bars are being closed down right, left, and centre. They can only be replaced by shops and restaurants. Can you imagine me running a boutique?

Sarah There are a lot of people worse off than you.

Brian That's no consolation. I have to face the fact that I'm finished unless I can find the cash to move. It's only a question of time. With my past lifestyle, there's not much left in the kitty. A bit more cash would keep me going a little longer.

Sarah Is that how you want to live? Do anything, so that your bar will keep going a little longer?

Brian Please go.

Sarah (*pleading*) Come with me.

Brian I'll be all right. I can look after myself.

Sarah You can't—that's the tragedy.

Sarah exits dejected

Mike Women. Too soft to get anywhere in this world.

Brian sits at table R

Brian Oh, shut up, can't you?

Mike Temper. (*He gets up*) I think I'll join you in a beer now. Like one?

Brian She's a good girl, Sarah. I can imagine how she feels if her husband was a heroin addict. Unlike you, some people do care about their fellow human beings.

Mike Like alcoholics?

Brian That's not the same thing.

Mike Really? I guess that is why you have no qualms about selling your drugs. Let's try some, shall we?

Mike exits. Presently, he returns with two beers

Brian Is it wise to get me drunk if you want me to drive to Bangkok?

Mike (*joining him at the table*) It's probably safer on Thai roads to be drunk. Sober, you wouldn't attempt it. Anyway, we won't go until it gets dark.

Brian Alcohol is legal. Heroin isn't. That's the difference between me and you.

Mike At the beginning of the century it was. They thought it was such a hero that they changed the original name. Interesting, isn't it, where they drew the line. Which drugs are acceptable and which are not. Funny thing is, governments make more money out of legal drugs than we do out of illegal ones.

Brian Why do you keep telling me all this?

Mike To educate you. To put you in the picture. To give you the opportunity to make an informed decision.

Brian Nobody makes an informed decision about smuggling heroin.

Mike They do. Not about the moral or historical position perhaps, but they have to weigh up the risk against the reward.

Brian To see if they are greedy enough.

Mike Sound like Sarah.

Brian She is right, isn't she?

Mike What is right? If people are stupid enough to take drugs when they've been warned of the consequences, whose fault is that? If they want to kill themselves, let them. The world's overpopulated anyway; perhaps it's nature's way of reducing it.

Brian You believe that?

Mike It's what you believe that counts.

Brian Why did I have to get here so early, if you want to wait until dark?

Mike Because I knew you'd need some convincing about the cargo. Also, I enjoy a good philosophical conversation. Not a lot of opportunity for this sort of chat in the jungle.

Brian You weren't very keen to chat before Sarah came.

Mike I'm more relaxed now. I didn't know things were going to work out so well.

Brian I haven't said yes yet.

Mike You will.

Brian How did you get involved in all this?

Mike In Cambodia, with the SAS, helping Prince Sihanouk's mob. When the fuss blew up that we were supposedly helping the Khmer Rouge too, we were forced to pull out. Instead of going home, I took up an offer to go independent.

Brian Become a mercenary.

Mike Freelance military adviser for the Shan army in Burma. It was there that I came to the attention of Khun Sa. He likes to boast he entered the drug trade to finance the battle for Shan independence. Well, it's as good a cover as any.

Brian He can't be very happy with you.

Mike Not overjoyed. I had become one of his trusted lieutenants, but it was time to get out. High risk work requires to be very lucrative, and, more importantly, very short term.

Brian How much have you got?

Mike Twenty kilos. Worth two hundred grand each on the streets of London, more if it's specially cut and given a few additives.

Brian That's four million!

Mike Only a drop in the ocean to Khun Sa. He sent one hundred and fifty tons out of The Golden Triangle last year. But his pride will be hurt, and I've got a few days before he finds out. So we don't want to leave any tracks. However, a chance in a lifetime for you. Take it to London, and earn a hundred grand.

Brian (*springing from his chair*) Take it to London!

Mike It's OK. I've organised these trips a hundred times. I know the system inside out.

Brian (*moving away*) Then why don't you take it?

Mike   Khun Sa's people are going to be watching the airport until they think I've got away. That'll mean weeks, maybe a couple of months. The longer we hide the heroin in Bangkok, the better chance they have of finding it. It can't be sold because this brand is too recognisably his; even Sarah knew that. It's like fruit: we have to get it to the market before it perishes; or we perish.

Brian   What's all this "we" business? It seems I'm the one doing everything.

Mike   The most difficult part was getting out of Laos. I did that. You don't have to do anything. You can walk away if you want. I'm offering you a chance to earn a hundred grand in a few days. It's up to you: take it or leave it.

Brian   (*joining him at the table*) If I say "Yes", how do I get it to London?

Mike   We have two identical cases. One perfectly normal, one with the heroin. You check in the normal case, and someone else checks in the heroin one.

Brian   Who?

Mike   I'll find someone, it's not difficult. I've had up to nine couriers on one flight. It's like Russian roulette for them at the other end. Sometimes we lay odds on which one will get caught.

Brian   And what would my odds be?

Mike   Very good. It's different when it's your own money.

Brian   How will I know who this other courier is?

Mike   I'll show you a photograph before you leave for the airport. However, don't make any contact with them at all. At Heathrow, they will leave the case on the carousel and only take through their hand luggage. Once they have cleared customs, you pick up the heroin case and walk through. If you are stopped, your real case is still on the carousel: you've picked up the wrong one. If your fingerprints are not on anything inside the heroin case, they can't connect it with you at all. The real smuggler panicked when you picked up his case by mistake.

Brian How do I know which case is which?

Mike Apart from looking at the labels, the heroin case will have an unobtrusive scratch on it.

Brian It's as simple as that.

Mike Works every time. The most dangerous part is getting the case out of Bangkok, but that's not your problem.

Brian And I get a hundred grand for this?

Mike In whatever currency you like.

Brian Who from?

Mike You'll be met at Heathrow by a friend of mine.

Brian How will I know he won't double-cross me?

Mike You don't trust anybody, do you?

Brian You haven't shown much trust in me.

Mike More than you imagine.

Brian Funny way of showing it.

Mike You have a bank account in Malaysia?

Brian Yes. Penang.

Mike I'll get my friend to transfer fifty thousand pounds into your account before you leave, and the other half on receipt of the goods. Fair enough?

Brian I suppose so. I don't know. I'm still not sure. It seems too easy.

Mike It is easy if you don't do anything stupid, or get unlucky.

Brian I've got to think about it.

Mike I'll give you a couple of hours. If you don't want to go, I'll find someone else. Pity though: I've already got you a flight booked for next Wednesday. (*He hands him a ticket*)

Brian (*getting up*) Singapore Airlines?

Mike What's the problem?

Brian They don't fly direct to Heathrow.

Mike No, you have to change in Singapore.

Brian (*alarmedly*) Don't they hang drug smugglers in Singapore?

Mike That's why you are going.

Brian What?

Mike To make it even safer at Heathrow. You are in no danger. Changing planes doesn't involve going through customs, and a direct flight from Singapore to Heathrow is even less likely to draw attention. They assume the mandatory death sentence will deter the smugglers.

Brian You've got it all worked out, haven't you?

Mike If you get caught, I lose my pension.

Brian (*giving back the ticket*) I've got to go for a walk and think about this.

Mike It's nowhere near here.

Brian What?

Mike The heroin. In case you were thinking of trying something stupid.

Brian I am thinking of trying something stupid. Flying to Singapore with twenty kilos of heroin is stupid.

Brian exits

Mike prepares to pay his bill

Sarah enters from the garden R

Sarah Why is he going to Singapore?

Mike What are you doing here?

Sarah (*forcefully*) Why is he going to Singapore?

Mike (*recovering*) We are not supposed to be seen together.

Sarah He was supposed to go to Heathrow.

Mike There has been a change of plan.

Sarah What change?

Mike A change to bring a higher profile. More publicity. Home Office figures are up and more action is required.

Sarah How are they going to achieve that?

Mike (*getting up*) By a hanging.

Sarah A what?

Mike Stuff about death row. Appeals for clemency. All that. Plenty of mileage for the taxpayer without Heathrow grinding to a halt.

Sarah (*furiously*) And whose idea was this?

Mike Sort of joint decision, I think. The Thais are pretty peeved at all the bad publicity they are getting for doing our dirty work. Those two girls were the straw that broke the camel's back. They don't take too kindly to being called barbarians and having hordes of tabloid journalists trawling for whatever sleaze they can find, real or imaginary. I must say I do sympathize with them. We wouldn't like it if they did it to us.

Sarah So why not Heathrow?

Mike I suppose it's that old Chinese proverb: "Shoot one to control a thousand." Arrests at Heathrow only carry a few lines these days. Being remanded by Uxbridge magistrates doesn't have the same ring about it as being measured for the drop. This way we'll get TV crews, footage of previous hangings, documentaries, maybe even live reports from Kate Adie.

Sarah And Singapore doesn't mind?

Mike They don't know. That's the beauty of the plan. Poor old Brian unwittingly checks in the heroin case. Arrives in squeaky clean Singapore. Before they can fine him for not flushing the loo, a bomb threat for the London flight is received. Off comes all the baggage, and "Oh, look what I've found."

Sarah And if they don't find it?

Mike They will.

Sarah But if they don't?

Mike Then he strikes lucky and gets picked up at London as originally planned. Neat, I call it.

Sarah That's not what I'd call it.

Mike Perhaps not.

Sarah Why wasn't I told?

Mike Operational reasons.

Sarah What's that supposed to mean.

Mike You had already made contact. I felt it wouldn't be in the best interests.

Sarah You felt it wouldn't be in the best interests?

Mike I told you it was an operational decision.

Sarah Fully sanctioned?

Mike Of course. Take it as a compliment. You are getting so good at the grieving widow act that I have to keep upping ante. Without you I could have reeled him in for half as much.

Sarah The idea is that he should be given the opportunity to back out, be warned to what he is getting involved in, be alerted to the evils. Only after all that is he fair game.

Mike Has he any family?

Sarah I don't know. I doubt it.

Mike Pity. Nothing like a grieving family trotting out for several front pages and features.

Sarah That's sick.

Mike You know what the final request was? Aim for his arrest on a slow news day. Would you believe it? How am I supposed to know when they are going to get caught jumping into bed with each other.

Sarah This is not right.

Mike He has been warned. We've done everything by the book.

Sarah The book doesn't set a limit on the amount to be offered. The book doesn't say anything about people being hung for better publicity. Offer anyone in the UK a hundred grand and see how many jump at it. I'm beginning to wonder if we're any better than the people we are trying to stop. This was a good idea to start with, but it's getting out of hand.

Mike (*losing his temper*) And so is heroin addiction. Giving out free samples to hook kids into a life of theft and violence to satisfy their addiction. Because once they are hooked, very few have the strength and the will-power to escape the fatal downward spiral. Do you want twelve-year olds dealing in schools, like in America? Because I don't. In my book, it's worth the death of a dozen Brians if we can prevent that. This is no ordinary product. Once the customer dies, they go and find someone else to hook. "Problems with your parents, problems with your girlfriend, problems with your school-work—take this. This will make them all go away and make you feel warm and happy." It's like buying an incurable disease. It is an evil. An evil that we have to protect our kids from by means fair or foul.

Sarah So the ends justify the means.

Mike does not answer

This stinks, you know, this really stinks.

Mike Look, if he says "No", I'll let him go. But if he says "Yes", I don't think he'll be much of a loss to the world. He'll be no different from the petty criminals we catch already. They are all Brians. Now I'm going for a wash, and you better make yourself scarce.

Mike exits

Sarah goes to sit at the table L. *She lights up a cigarette, for a few moments contemplating what to do*

Brian enters, looking for his hold-all, which is still under the chair at table R. *He notices Sarah*

Brian Come back?

Sarah (*thinking quickly*) Ah... The plane had already left.

Brian Is there another one?

Sarah In a few hours.

Brian Come for one final shot at persuading me not to go?

Sarah Nowhere else to go.

Brian Oh, I see.

Sarah Decided?

Brian Sorry.

Sarah Going?

Brian No choice.

Sarah Sure?

Brian Yes.

Sarah Pity.

Brian (*joining her at the table*) You know, I admire you.

Sarah I can't think why.

Brian I told Mike you were a loser. But walking around just now I came to the conclusion that I was the loser. If I wasn't, I wouldn't consider going with him. You must have much worse financial problems than me, but you wouldn't even consider it, would you?

Sarah You still don't have to.

Brian (*getting up*) I do. I love this country too much. I couldn't go back home now, I'd rather die here. What is someone my age going to do in England? I can't go back to the cabs—I'd get lost. If I have to stay, I might as well be in jail as anywhere.

Sarah Haven't you any family?

Brian Not really. My mother died last year. I've no real relatives left. My family is here.

Sarah Here?

Brian My girls. My bar-girls. A great bunch, always smiling, laughing at the smallest thing. And what have they got to be happy about? They come from the poor rural parts of the country where the average wage is little over a hundred pounds a year. They work in the bars in Pattaya for a couple of months to earn enough money to return to their families and buy a buffalo or a pig. Is that wrong?

Sarah (*getting up*) Millions of girls here don't do that.

Brian True, but they were born here. I have to leave the country every three months to renew my visa, keep the creditors from my door, pay the police if they catch me working. That is my buffalo.

Sarah But you could scrape by.

Brian Perhaps, but the future for someone like me is very uncertain. I'm not as strong as you. It scares me. This opportunity could be my last chance. One flight which will keep me going for life. Even if they rip me off at Heathrow, I'll still have fifty grand in the bank in Penang. I'll make sure you get your money back. Double. No, triple.

Sarah (*trying not to look at him*) Don't worry about it.

Brian But I do. It's not your fault all this happened, it's mine. I'm a prat, as you said, but I'll be back on the first flight, no worries. Sorry, sound like an Aussie backpacker. Penalty of being surrounded by so many. Anyway, until I can pay you back, I want you to have something. A sort of deposit, but you can keep it. Supposed to bring good luck. Might be better for you. (*He takes off his necklace with the golden Buddha and hands it to her*)

Sarah No, I can't. I really can't.

Brian (*forcing it into her hand*) Please, it would make me very happy. I know you like it. If I get caught, it'll only end up as part of Her Majesty's property, and she's got enough jewellery already. Better you keep it. You can give it back when I return, if you want.

Sarah Thanks.

Brian (*breaking away from her*) Do you know where Mike is?

Sarah Gone for a wash.

Brian I'd better go and find him. (*He moves to the exit*)
Sarah (*calling out*) Brian.
Brian Yes.

Sarah goes to sit on the edge of table R. *She looks at him, then at the Buddha in her hand*

Sarah (*after a long pause*) Nothing.
Brian See you later then.

Brian exits, leaving Sarah sitting on the edge of the table, staring at the Buddha. She holds up the chain

Sarah Perhaps. (*She drops the chain in the palm of her hand*)

The Lights fade

CURTAIN

FURNITURE AND PROPERTY LIST

On stage: Various plants
Spirit house with Buddha statues
White table. *On it:* beer bottles
2nd table
4 chairs
Hold-all. *In it:* newspaper (*Bangkok Post* or *The Nation*)

Off stage: 2 beers (**Mike**)

Personal: **Mike:** cigarettes, wrist-watch, Singapore Airlines ticket
Brian: necklace with a golden Buddha
Sarah: cigarettes, passport and other papers

LIGHTING PLOT

Property fittings required: nil
Exterior. The same throughout

To open: General lighting

Cue 1   **Sarah** drops the chain in the palm of her hand   (Page 27)
         Fade lights

PRINTED BY
THE KINGFISHER PRESS, LONDON NW10 6UG